IN THE FOOTSTEPS OF POETS

inspired by Clevedon

Also from Clevedon Community Press

Writing on the Lake: an anthology of poetry and prose, 2016.
ISBN: 978-0-9935666-0-8

Jane Lilly
Clevedon Cuttings: history, houses and a couple of characters, 2017.
ISBN: 978-0-9935666-1-5

John Birkinshaw
Celebrating Portishead Open Air Pool, 2018.
ISBN: 978-0-99356666-2-2

IN THE
FOOTSTEPS
OF POETS

Clevedon Community Press

ISBN: 978-0-9935666-3-9

First published 2019 by
Clevedon Community Press
Unit 15, Tweed Road Estate
Clevedon BS21 6RR

Cover design: Rob Donachie
Pen & ink centre map: Stephanie Fitch
Photographs: Eleanor Wade and Peter Gibbs
Printed and bound by: bookprintinguk

Acknowledgements

We thank Peter Gibbs whose poems are published in this collection. Peter approached us to express his interest in the Clevedon Community Press publishing his work on iconic aspects of Clevedon – places that those walking the footpaths and pavements of Clevedon might come across. Peter very generously agreed to the Bookshop Co-operative inviting others in Clevedon to contribute to such an anthology. The outcome is this delightful and varied collection of poems all 'inspired by Clevedon'. Thank you to all our poets!

And we thank all those who have given their time, using their talents, to help produce *In the Footsteps of Poets*: Rob Donachie for his captivating book cover and ThatCopyShop for help with formatting this; Stephanie Fitch for her pen and ink sketch map of Clevedon; our book reviewers; and Professor David Punter for his support and advice.

A truly co-operative writing project!

The Publishing Press Team
Clevedon Community Bookshop Co-operative

CONTENTS

A Sonnet for Clevedon

Sea-licked, sun-dressed, Curzon-flicked, pier-blessed,
Bowling-greened, poet-walked, film-scened,
swallow-hawked,
Hill-Roaded, Dial-Hilled, car-loaded, space-filled,
Change-averse, pub-shorn, commuter-cursed,
fog-horned,
Yeo-threaded, tree-bent, flower-bedded, well-meant,
Triangled, Betjeman-praised, star-spangled,
heat-hazed,
Buzzard-crossed, sky-kissed, storm-tossed, bus-missed,
Walton-Castled, green-binned, seldom-hassled,
Ettlingen-twinned,
Clock-towered, street-proud, salt-soured,
Elton-endowed,
Cricket-pitched, motorway-served, café-rich,
coast-curved,
Liam-Foxed, Ladye-Bayed, hard-rocked, got-it-made,
Bandstanded, Marine-Laked, broadbanded,
Pullin-baked,
Bargeboarded, Coleridge-veiled, shed-recorded,
Highdaled,
Tide-surged, sunset-cheered, Broadchurched,
wind-seared.

 Poet – Robin Kidson

Poets' Coastal Way

Skirting, the outer edge.
Snaking, a hill top church.
Nestled, inside its thorny hedge.
Protected from incoming seaward storms.

Onwards along cliffs high,
hovering birds of prey cry.
Dropping down; boats recline.
Weathered and worn, in decline.

Trailing allotments catch the light,
from lingering western skies;
settling, warm and bright,
on old cemetery walls.

Just beyond the town's reach,
an outer spinal tidal beach.
Reappears when tides are low.
On the daily ebb and flow.

Did those poets walk this way,
in earlier times; before –
and watch the lowering sun,
spread golden across the shore.

 Poet - Sally Cornelius

Clevedon Meanderings

Sun shining
Across the carpet
Walking boots snarl
In the hall, too long still
Draw of fresh air
Pulls me off
The comfy chair.

Whether fleece, hat and gloves
Or T-shirt and sunscreen
Always booted, I stride
Across the threshold.
Turn and click
The key in the lock.

Up the drive, turn right
There lie the crossways of choice.
Seasonal whisperings overheard
Glimpse fitful sights,
As murmurings unfurl.
Where best to go meandering………?

 **Poet – Eleanor Wade**

THE PIER

Location on map .. *1*

Clevedon Pier

A thing of beauty;
Ethereal silhouette
Against a burnished sky,
A phantom in mists that
Whisper with a million footsteps,
A ribbon of soft globes lighting
The black of night,
A sunlit promenade
Alive with voices and laughter.

Pounded by gales and towering waves,
Lashed by rains driven in from the West,
Buffeted by tides that race, deep and fast,
Supported by curves that embrace the storm.

The storehouse of twelve thousand names,
It touches the past, slows down time,
Celebrates memories, refreshes the soul,
Allows for dreams.

 Poet – Bernie Jordan

A Pier Without Peer

Graceful iron arches
Have spanned one fifty years
This famous Clevedon landmark
Most beautiful of piers

Victorian designers
Made use of Brunel's rails
To craft this classic landing stage
For steamer trips from Wales

Pagoda at its pierhead
A toll house on the land
Opened then to much acclaim
With cannons and massed band

Countless generations
Have strolled its weathered boards
While anglers watch their lines in hope
Ignoring summer hordes

Collapse in 1970 –
That might have spelt the end
When those who lacked the vision said,
It is too dear to mend

John Betjeman its saviour
Knight Poet Laureate
He fought its demolition –
A most unworthy fate

And so the spans were raised anew
Our civic pride regained
For yet unborn Clevedonians
An asset now retained

Some piers they may be longer
And others labelled Grand
But Clevedon holds the title
Of fairest in the land.

 **Poet – Peter Gibbs**

Cruising on the Balmoral

Underneath a mackerel sky, Balmoral reached the pier

And those who knew her secret shed a hidden tear

Was this the last from Clevedon to head off out to Wales?

The end of her proud history? The last of many tales?

Penarth's pierhead was crowded by Welsh there for the cruise

The loyal and the faithful, though most had heard the news

Of cancelled trips and mishaps, of parts to be replaced

But though she'd faced some stormy seas, she never was disgraced

Now the day turned sunny as out across the foam

She headed back for Somerset past isles of Steep and Holm

Down the coast she voyaged beneath a dome of blue

Hills and harbours passing – a panoramic view

Minehead then to Lynmouth, now peaceful after flood

That turned a pretty village into a sea of mud

Past Woody Bay and towering cliffs - the tallest in the land

Balmoral sailed serenely on - a day out she'd made grand

At Ilfracombe a welcome - town crier there to say,

"We're very pleased to see you - o'yez, o'yez, o'yez!"

Some went ashore for lunching while others came aboard

Beneath the gaze of Verity – a sculpture some find flawed

And after streets to wander, the time to bid farewell

And set off from the quayside into the tidal swell

The journey home for chatting as golden sun went down

To give a vibrant light show - the cruise's final crown

Balmoral in the sunset - the worries for the morn

We hope she'll keep on cruising and find a bright, new dawn.

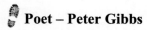 **Poet – Peter Gibbs**

50 Years of Waverley Voyages

We teuk the ferry, frae the Broomielaw
Doon the watter – wiz affie braw
A picnic and a wee bit cone
On the sun-kust isle where palm trees grew
And fishes flew? Wha knew?
That magic blae-skied Rothesay day
In Ayrshire's Mandalay.

We took the ferry, from Clevedon Pier,
One cold grey day – went all the way
Down the estuary
To enjoy the view for an hour or two
From wind-swept Lundy bays.
Where people say that seals and dolphin play
But not today.

A sandwich, ice-cream, cup of tea,
Then we were on our way.
Tide and paddle pushed us home.
With setting sun behind us,
Pink fronds fringed the grey
At Clevedon Pier pagoda
In Somerset's Mandalay.

 Poet – Grace Hewson

AT THE WATER'S EDGE

Location on the map .. *2*

Seafront

Trees bent, giving way to the wind

Pebbles. Treasure, from your hand to my pocket.
Rattling.

I've beaten this track many times.

As a child, visiting. As a couple, chips & a stroll.

As an exhausted new mum, pram gripped tightly.
Pushing. Pushing. Pushing.

Sitting on a bench.

The peace and view a saviour. A balm for my weary
soul.

 Poet – Alexandra Bridger

Breakfast at The Beach

Eggs with skill light-scrambled
At Number Five The Beach
Create so fine a breakfast
That one is lost for speech
With salmon smoked and bagel
Served on a large, hot plate
A table by the window –
Pier view to contemplate
Smiling, friendly service
Make this a meal complete
An early morning bonus –
Another Clevedon treat.

Marine Lake Swimmers

All hail the early bathers
Swimwear on before the dawn
Then entering the water
As autumn day is born
Mirrored surface broken
As 'cross the lake they power
Immune they to the coldness
At this the waking hour
They say it's warmer in there
Than standing on the brink
But some are made for swimming
While others merely sink.

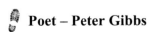 **Poet – Peter Gibbs**

Clevedon Pier to Poets' Walk and Back

There's a windy walk I know very well
Along the seafront from the Pier
Where swimmers splash and brave the swell

Past bandstand where trees are bent with pain
Weave through a mini wood, and out again

Past The Harp – a quick drink here
Fancy some wine or maybe a beer?

The amusement arcade, drag the children right past
Oh no! There's fish and chips, what shall we do?
Have some now and take in the view?

The massive sea wall divides sea from lake
Swimmers, zorbers and paddle boarders too
Crowded when sunny, how to get through?

Out to the viewpoint then up to the lookout
How many first kisses were stolen inside?
How many yesses to make her the bride?

Off up the wilder bit, left up Church Hill
A zigzag, we're breathless, a seat at the top
We finally make it, feeling a thrill

A breathtaking view, I've seen before
Uplifting as ever, I can see for miles
I come away breathing nothing but smiles

Along to Wain's Hill
Overlooking The Pill
A flash of a peregrine passes by
– 200 mile an hour plummet from the sky –

There's mud for miles, waders too
Little boats tilt, wait for their cue

Past allotments, through woods to the glebe
A peaceful place, where those that grieve
Plant trees, leave notes, or sit awhile

The landward path of green arched trees
Leads to Salthouse Fields and the ever present breeze.

 Poet – Jenny Bradley

Family of Three

Our first outing as a family of three.
We drove,
Everything a huge undertaking in those early days.

The sun beat down
Your skin hot and clammy against mine.
We meandered through the crowds.
The sound of the train startled you.
This bright, boisterous world a change from four walls
and my face.
We paused by the playground, a jolt of realisation
freezing me.
Would I push you on those swings?
A life outside feeding and sleep deprivation impossible
to grasp.

Flags on their poles danced to their own rhythm,
drawing us to the view.
I lifted you;
"There's Wales!"
You were captivated by the glistening water, murky
brown yet diamond bright.

We walked on.
You fell asleep on my shoulder.
Your warm, sweet breath moistening my neck.
Your heavy contentment.

We made it.
Our first outing as a family of three.

Poet – Alexandra Bridger

Sally's Clevedon Rainbow

An arc of perfect colours
Anchored in the sea
Promising two crocks of gold
And one I'll keep for thee
Above the pier where your plaque tells
Of love for Clevedon town
A sunshine-tinted garland
As soft rain filters down
November's chill just vanishes
Your warmth enfolds my heart
With Nature's joy to link us
We'll never be apart.

 **Poet – Peter Gibbs**

Kicking the Bar, midwinter

Trudge down the seafront,
Head down, hood up,
Paving strewn with bladderwrack
From the night's high tide.
Sidestep the puddles
In rain-spattered walking boots.
Brisk pace, long strides,
Alongside the grey, bedraggled sea
Tied tight to the solid curtain of cloud
Screening the hills beyond.
Keep going; it's not far
To the edge where sludgy fingers
Claw the rocky shore.
Then, when the fence says 'no more'
You've reached the end.
Toe-tap the bottom rail and head for home.
Not crossing, just kicking the bar.

 Poet – Grace Hewson

Note from the poet on Kicking the Bar:
As a child in Aberystwyth, I regularly joined the family to walk the length of the prom to 'kick the bar'. Now with our beautifully restored Marine Lake, I can do the same thing here. I am not the only one – there are always other muddy footprints on the bar. As opposed to Tennyson's 'Crossing the Bar' and Stevie Smith's 'Not Waving but Drowning', this is a poem, and walk, of determined self-preservation.

Note from the poet on Kicking the Bar continued …

I start from the pier, keeping straight on, admiring the bandstand, ignoring the amusement arcade, keeping to the upper level then dropping down to the far side of the lake, then returning at the lower level, across the narrow walkway with the water at either side, pausing, when weather is more favourable, to take in the view of the light on the water, the pier and the hills beyond.

Promenade Sunset

Neon shafts across the sky
Cloud strands shot through with fire
Nature's sunset miracle
The spent day's funeral pyre
Heavens slashed with colours
Crimson, orange, red
From the far horizon
Stretching overhead
The turning Earth extinguishes
The sun from Channel view
One final ray across a sea
Turned luminous in hue
Night falls upon the promenade
Edged with its garland lights
And strollers pause to wonder
At Clevedon's bonus sights.

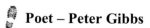 **Poet – Peter Gibbs**

Clevedon Sunset

Along the streets of stone-cast villas
Heavy with poetic muse
Paths of history leading seawards
To the bay of sunset views
Where giant fans of golden searchlights
Pierce the clouds of dark'ning grey
Catching ships within their broad sweep
As the dusk winds down the day
Through the bandstand's note-filled arches
Landscape artists' hues remain
On palettes formed from out the heavens
Reflecting down their pink-tinged stain
O'er the old pier's spans of iron
Hov'ring ducks ride zephyr trails
Heading out into the Channel
Silhouetted 'gainst far Wales
Pinpoint lights in looping garlands
Lead the eye to where Wains Hill
Towers above the travelling fairground
Candy floss and high-pitched thrill
Dodgem cars and swinging galleons
Hoopla stalls and music blare
That tempt the townsfolk out to wander
There the summer night to share.

 Poet – Peter Gibbs

The Lookout

Location on the map .. *3*

At the Look Out

Finzel sits in his look out tower,
Waiting for his ships to come out of the sky.
He counted them out and he'll count them back in,
A telescope fixed on to watery eye,
Leaving a permanent panda O,
Like the end of the barrel of a gun,
A zero, a wheel, a world, a sun.

Finzel waits in his look out tower,
Second to minute, minute to hour,
Watching the corrugations of the sea.
The path round the headland comes back to nought.
Poets walk in circles with little intent.
He has sugar and gold in profusion,
So why is he never completely content?

Finzel watches in his look out tower,
Tapping his sore and impatient feet,
Time is money, time is power,
Is time a circle or is it a line?
He watches as ships go out and come in,
None of them his, no profit in sight,
Time is passing, and time is tight.

Finzel sits in his look out tower,

Bounded by ivy and sycamore trees.

He wonders what sights this headland has seen:

Cabot on the lookout for new found land,

Privateers off to the Spanish Main,

The tainted ships sailing to Africa,

Triangular trade, round and round again.

 Poet – Robin Kidson

Note from the poet on At the Lookout:

Erected circa 1835 by Ferdinand Beeston. Said to have been used by the Finzel family, sugar importers in the mid 19th century, to view sugar ships coming from the West Indies.

Inscription on The Lookout, Poets Walk, Clevedon.

The Lookout

Look out through the arches. What do you see?
Three little fishing boats, bobbing lazily.
A cruise ship taking people hoping for some sun
And food and wine and dancing, a fortnight full of fun.
A container ship with cigarettes to sell in far-off lands
Or rubbish which we do not want to soil our British
hands.

Look back - those ships are taking young men off to
war,
Munitions, armaments and tanks head for a foreign
shore.
Look out at night when all is black; no light allowed to
shine
But moon and channel lead the way for the approaching
drone
Then flash and flame light up the sky, as distant
docklands burn.

Look back again and back once more.
The cargo ships are weighed down low.
Sugar cane, tobacco leaves,
Pass by to Bristol factories.
So splendid city buildings soar
And spacious villas line the estuary shore.
Look back, look back, look back before

The arches perched above the shore.
A tall mast ship sails out to sea.
What's in the hold? No-one can see
Men, women, children held in chains
Are bound for Caribbean plains.

 Poet – Grace Hewson

Note from the poet on The Lookout:
Near the beginning of the beautiful Poets' Walk, the cliff path around the edge of Church Hill and Wain's Hill, a folly called The Lookout was built in 1835, two years after the abolition of slavery in Britain. The plantations of the West Indies and America were still dependent on forced labour. Let us not forget that the wealth of Bristol's merchants which was responsible for Clevedon's splendid Georgian and Victorian architecture, had foundations full of dirty secrets.

Poets' Walk to The Pill

Location on the map .. *4*

Clevedon Bay

And we came at last to the river's mouth
Where the banks stood far apart
And a small town nestled on a curving bay
And its beauty warmed my heart.

The tide was high gainst the legs of a Pier
Graceful child of times long gone
And the waves swept in across three bays
Splashed gold by the setting sun.

Lining the shore and climbing the hills
Bright houses faced the breeze
Around to the headland where poets once walked
And a church hid among the trees.

But the tide took us on round those ancient rocks,
Past the boats moored safe in the Pill.
Long I gazed back and I vowed to return;
And I do - for I love it still.

 Poet – Bernie Jordan

The Happy Brambler

I love to go a-brambling
Along the Poets' Walk
And as I go I sometimes sing
But hardly ever talk

Val-deri, val-dera
Val-deri, val-dera
Ha, ha, ha, ha, ha, ha
Val-deri, val-dera
I hardly ever talk

If walkers ever ask me
I tell them what I do
I'm helping out the group called Friends
And they say, Good on you

Val-deri, val-dera
Val-deri, val-dera
Ha, ha, ha, ha, ha, ha
Val-deri, val-dera
And they say, Good on you

I snip off all the spiky shoots
But leave the pretty flowers
For blackberries will soon appear
As long as we have showers

Val-deri, val-dera
Val-deri, val-dera
Ha, ha, ha, ha, ha, ha
Val-deri, val-dera
As long as we have showers

 Poet – Peter Gibbs

Note from the poet on The Happy Brambler:
'the group called Friends' is the volunteer group who keep
the area tidy – the Friends of Poets Walk.

The Gentle Hills of Genteel Clevedon

I walked the gentle hills of genteel Clevedon
I ambled pleasantly along Poet's Walk
Strangers with dogs exchanging small talk
And enjoying the sights of this sunny day,
Smiling courteously as we let each other pass
While the earth as we know it suffocates
Poisoned by plastic and waste
Pollution and corruption
While sea levels rise
And animals become extinct
As the earth grows hotter and hotter,

We amble pleasantly along the gentle hills of genteel
Clevedon

Hemmed in by culture and denial

And positive dispositions

Oh let us be more like Sheela Na Gig on the side of
Saint Andrews church

Spread our legs

Entertain the disagreeable

And stop being so bloody genteel

 Poet – Wendy Martineau

Rainbow Over Clevedon Pill

Steadily the tide comes in
To meet the shore again
Crossing 'neath a shining arch
Where sunshine paints the rain
The mud that lines the hidden creek
Is soon to disappear
As water fills the channels
And anchored boats swing clear
Across Black Rock the curlews sound
Their haunting clarion cry
As egrets pace and herons watch
And gulls take to the sky

 Poet – Peter Gibbs

In the footsteps of Poets

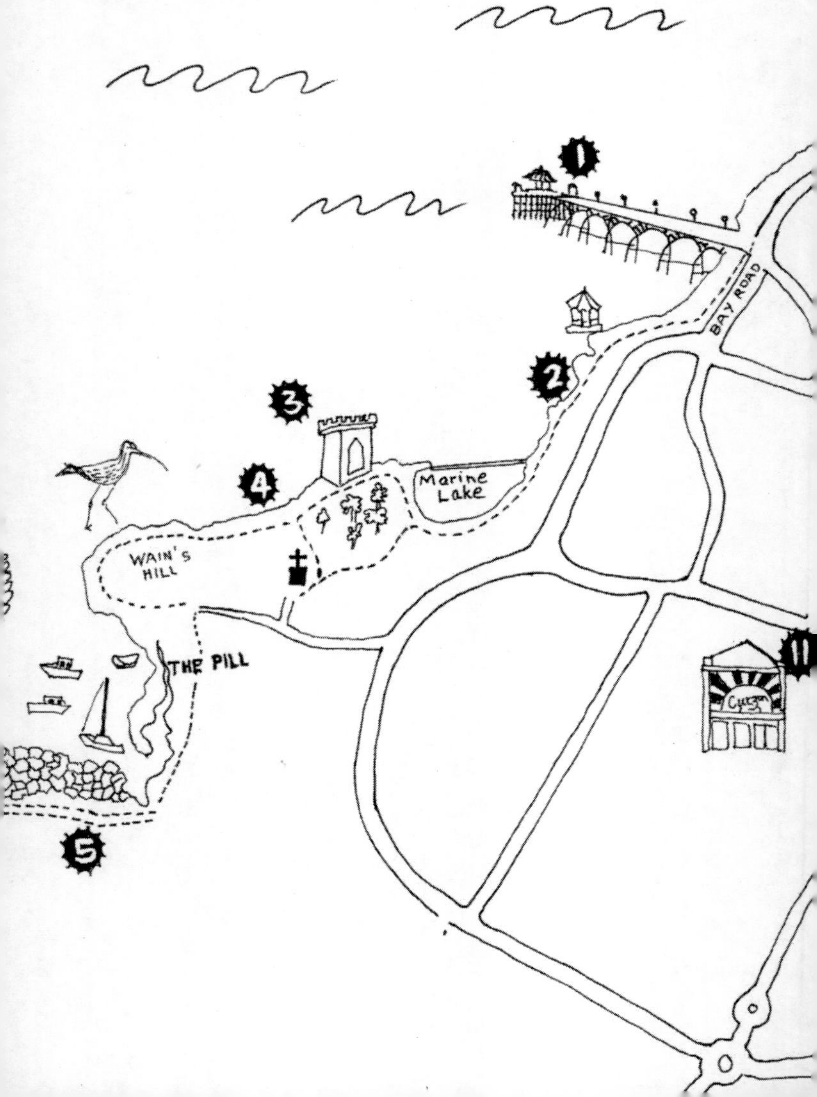

Marine Lake

BAY ROAD

WAIN'S HILL

THE PILL

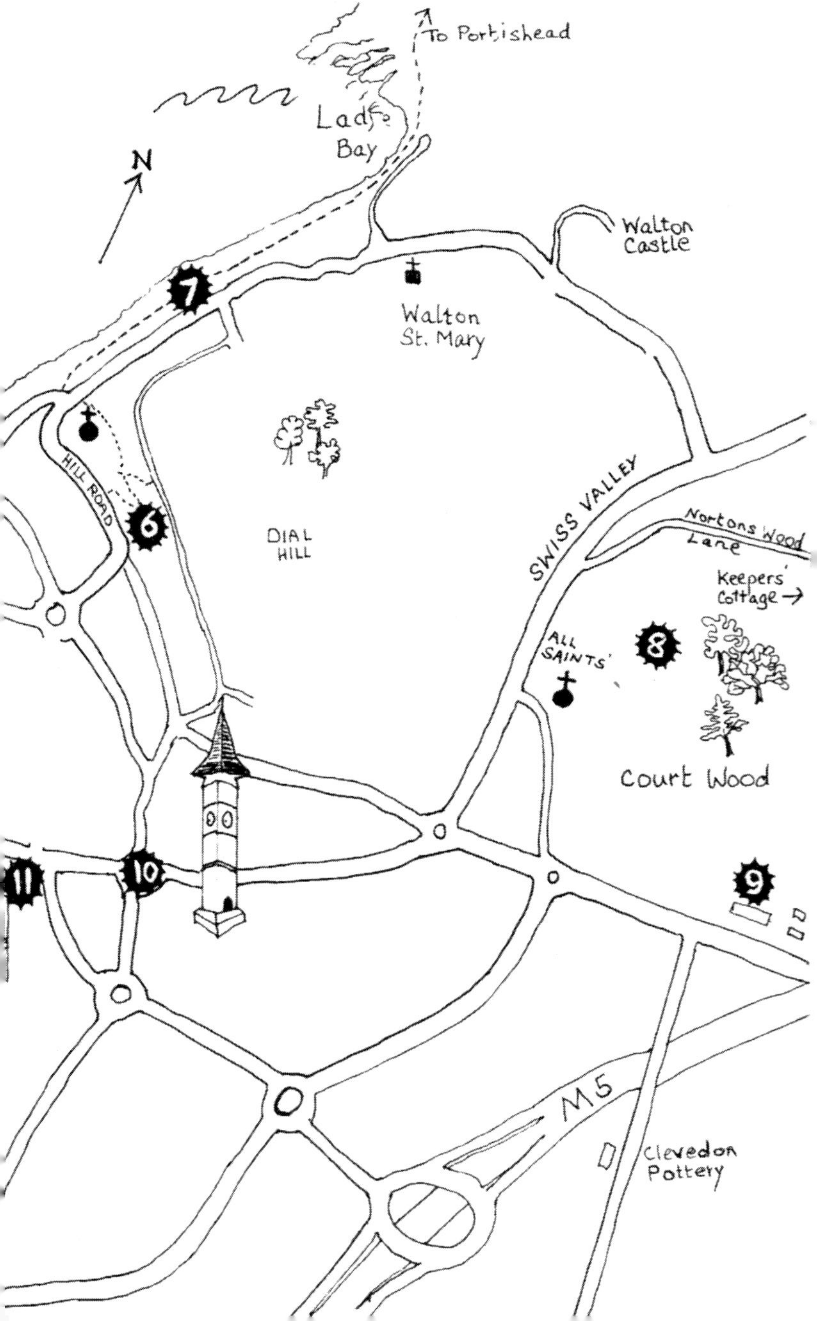

To Portishead

Ladye Bay

N

Walton Castle

Walton St. Mary

7

Hill Road

6

DIAL HILL

SWISS VALLEY

Nortons Wood Lane

Keepers' Cottage →

8

ALL SAINTS'

Court Wood

10

11

9

M5

Clevedon Pottery

Walk for Inspiration

Blow wind blow
Crack your cheeks
No wonder poets came here
Tennyson, Coleridge, Thackeray
Honeymooned in cottages
Stayed in grand houses
To write, to breathe, to feel the air

As the light goes
Over The Pill
An eerie blink of light
A lone boat tended by a skipper
Mud ripples in daylight
Stirring thoughts to match
Heavy stickiness, supplier of life

Large open skies show space and hope
River empties into estuary
Feeding, feeding, that great mass of water
Throwing itself up and down
Bristol Channel twice a day

Wonder of the waves retreating
From that shingle beach
Further, further, further

Revealing sandbank after sandbank
No wonder writers were inspired
To scrawl on paper
Perched on a walking stick

And behind, in the field
A forming, freezing, increasing pool as winter deepens
Fills with lapwing, shelduck, mallard and more
Narrow path needs boots and galoshes now
Bushes have shed their blackberries, hips and haws

Along the little lane, the quiet river bank
Enticing for a summer picnic stop
Serene waters to walk home by
To put down another poem, or two.

 Poet – Jenny Bradley

Note from the poet on Walk for Inspiration:
It is said that Coleridge honeymooned at 55 Old Church
Road, Clevedon.

Harvest Moon

Moon across the Channel
Competing with the dawn
Golden lantern in the sky
As the new day's born
Reflecting in the waters
Round painted bobbing boats
Pink tinged the east horizon
As o'er the sea she floats
All too soon she vanishes
This mistress of the tides
Gone to seek the evening
As up the brash sun glides.

 Poet – Peter Gibbs

Seawall

Location on the map .. 5

Sea Wall Birding

Walking out to Dowlais
On sea-defensive wall
Looking for the waders
Awaiting curlews call

Lapwing and spotted redshank
Beneath the heron's gaze
Swallows skimming water
Foretelling summer days

Pippits 'tween the boulders
Wheatears flashing by
A background soaring chorus
As larks ascend to sky

From out the tide-washed grassland
Goldfinches taking wing
As up along the fence wires
The linnets gaily sing

Incoming tide to gather
Shelduck and dunlin flocks
Oyster catchers seeking
Their food among the rocks

On Clevedon's open shoreline
United in the sun
Residents and migrants
Enjoying Spring as one

 Poet – Peter Gibbs

The Zig Zag

Location on the map .. *6*

Those Zigzag Days

Walking up and down the Zigzag
was our childhood route,
to and from the town,
we did in all winds and weathers,
the whole year around.

Our home was up on Dial Hill,
all the shops were in the town,
we all had our bicycles,
but it was a long way round by road,
so up and down that Zigzag path,
every day we three kids strode.

Yes up and down that Zigzag,
to fetch shopping for our mum,
walking up was jolly hard,
but going down was fun,
tearing around all those corners,
on a top to bottom run.

Be careful children you'll stumble,
and then you'll take a tumble,
and if you knock an old lady down,
be sure there'll be a grumble.

Yes up and down that Zigzag,
from early morning till late at night,
jumping out on Mum and Dad
and giving them both a fright.

It was our way to the pictures,
twice on Saturday we'd go,
home for lunch carrying fish and chips,
and then back for the afternoon show,

Yes running down that Zigzag,
to play in the Hill Road park,
and if it was deep winter,
we'd not get back till dark.

Those Zigzag days,
were carefree times,
when we kids were free to roam,
then toiling up that curving path
the gateway to our home.

 Poet – Nigel Heath

Zig-Zag Sunday

By Old Park House where centuries
Have passed the white-washed wall
A carven post and verdant paths echo the Dial Hill call
From flower-strewn lofty vantage point
Above the slumbering bay
The dawn-eyed watcher scans the hills and fondly
greets the day
Down the Zig-Zag to the town,
Lit by the brightening sun
The early walker strides along with nature linked as one
No company but slug and snail,
No sounds but wind and bird
A Sunday symphony of life not by the sleepers heard

He savours each new vista
As his route it gently drops
To Hill Road's regal line-up of shuttered silent shops
Past mansions bathed in sunlight
Bellevue and Elton Roads
Past banks and lovers' letters waiting sorting by their
codes
And then the promenade along
The sea-defending wall
In sight of the Victorian pier that waits the steamer's
call

Past trees bent back by Welsh-sent winds

And bandstand locked in time

Past white gulls foraging in mud, past bins upturned by crime

The flags of nations catch the breeze

Alongside Salthouse Field

Where giddy rollercoaster rides sit covered and concealed

Across train tracks and waiting swings

From out the trees there swells

To call the faithful to their prayers, a summoning of bells

And then the climb up Poets' Walk

Where others strolled before

To look upon the waters deep where galleons ply no more

He turns and sees old Clevedon

Set proudly on display

Beneath the hill where he began his happy Zig-Zag way.

 Poet – Peter Gibbs

In Search of a Viewpoint

And when you've had your fill
Of coffee shops and birthday cards
Head up the hill
You'll have to walk up Zigzag path
Or climb the steps tucked in behind
The Lime House rubbish bins.
Keep on and up and round the bend
Then pause for breath, sit on a bench
Or lean on the fence
To gaze above the shops
Across the Georgian chimneytops
To Sand Point, Steepholm, Flatholm and beyond.

But that's not all
Continue up and round then take
The narrow stony path beside the wall
With little wooden inset doors to secret worlds.
Wild Celery, Cow Parsley, Alexanders lead the way
To tempting tussocks where you can stand
To look across the bay
But do not stay!

Just walk along a few yards more
Before the path drops down and tarmac takes a right,
There, on the left,
Above another tiny stone-arched gate,
A tall Scots pine delineates the view,
Reaching majestically in the blue
Toward the church bell tower,

The delicate finger of pier
Hazily pointing out to sea.

There, that's the spot.
Stand still
Set up your camera
And take the shot.

 Poet – Grace Hewson

Note from the poet on In Search of a Viewpoint:
Starting from Hill Road, this walk is explained within the poem. Once at the viewpoint, walkers can continue down the path to Wellington Terrace. Cross over the road then turn left for the pier and more coffee shops or turn right along Lovers Lane to Ladye Bay and beyond, even all the way to Portishead.

Coastal Path

Location on the map .. *7*

Clevedon's Best-Kept Secret

I face Marine Place
Where modern meets old,
As these houses on stilts
Obscure the view into the past
To Victorian Clevedon.

For that I must continue
Up the unassuming path,
Until the bushes part,
Revealing a harmonious combination
Of steel and wood
That Betjeman so admired.

Further on I go,
Greeted by dog-walkers, joggers, lovers,
Where bees buzz in summer
And blackberries blossom in autumn.
This narrow, muddy path
Navigating the sheer cliff
Which the hotel clings to.

Then I reach some steps
And I am breathless,
Not from exertion but wonder
As the estuary, so tranquil,
Reaches out before me to the Welsh hills,

While the pier stands majestically: the jewel in the crown.

I descend some distance
To find a rocky shore:
Clevedon's best-kept secret
Where toddlers collect stones,
Children hunt crabs
And teenagers 'hang out.'

Barbecue smoke and cannabis coalesce
Where generations meet
To while away the day
In secluded Ladye Bay
Until the tide chases us away.

 Poet – Jenni Jackson

Roger's Seat – Clevedon Coastal Path

On Roger's seat the world's at peace
Upon this summer's day
The coastal path still beckons
But I'm inclined to stay

Across the Channel's Newport
Before its misty hills
In front the gently turning blades
Of modern power windmills

Dark cormorants skim the muddy waves
A sparrowhawk darts by
And oystercatchers take to wing
To trail their piping cry

And then at last reluctantly
I follow on my way
That winds past rocky beaches
To end at Ladye Bay.

 Poet – Peter Gibbs

History in a Hamlet

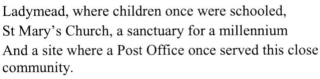

Walton St Mary
Lies up on Castle Hill,
A collection of history;
Ladymead, where children once were schooled,
St Mary's Church, a sanctuary for a millennium
And a site where a Post Office once served this close
community.

Where Castle Road curves
Sits a gate which opens
Into a sea of green,
Climbing up you may spot
A poised golfer taking aim
Or a timid stag staring, bewildered by your intrusion.

You reach secluded cottages
And standing before you is the nineteenth hole
But this journey is not over;

Through an unsuspecting gate
You wade through mud
Emerging
To a breathtaking panorama.

The epitome of tranquillity;
The Severn Bridge so serene,
Traversed by the Prince of Wales,
Where England and Wales meet,
This cable-stayed construction,
Illuminated by the setting sun.

If you stay a while
You may catch a ship,
These mammoth vessels
Glide by at speed,
Travelling the final furlong,
Carrying cargo from distant lands,
When the tide is right.

As the light fades,
You retrace your steps,
Greeted by a glimpse
Of the seventeenth century;
A castle restored
Where wedding vows are made
And you pledge to return.

 Poet – Jenni Jackson

Estuary Views

In the woods behind Clevedon School, upward
To find the top of The Ripple path
Cross into another path held in place by houses
Straight in front; is Channel Road – part one
The Avenue slices through like a knife
Over again into Channel Road – part two

Onward to where
A Royal Mail post box stands sentinel
By a small gate into St Mary's Church
Dawdle through, admire the gardening
Read the gravestones
Standing guard over those lingering in eternity
Passing the bell tower; see where old meets new
Out of the night black lych gate.

Bay Road sees estuary views
Destinations leftwards lead to the Coastal Path
Drift down any
To find a place to stand, to gaze
At the wonder of millions on millions
Of accumulated molecules washing to-and-fro
Gallons of liquid that travel the world
Can fly through the sky as clouds
Fall as rain and start the cycle again.

 **Poet – Eleanor Wade**

Woodland

Location on map .. *8*

In Court Woods

Nobody knows I'm here
Perched on the log seat
Behind the tree
A cloak of shade and silence at my back
Ahead, a near sheer drop,
The gold-tinged valley spread below.
How did I get here?
I don't quite know
I've never been the same way twice
Paths just draw me upwards
Zigzagging between the trees, scrambling up scree
To the magic ring of beech,
Once a perfect circle,
Now invaded by rogue sycamores.
Past narrow rhododendron aisles
On to the broad sweep
Fit for ladies riding from the manor house.
Eyes peeled for the little path which runs
Like a fox through tangled grass.
Then pause awhile on that log seat
So thoughtfully placed for afternoon adventurers
To sit and dream of worlds beyond.

 Poet – Grace Hewson

Note from the poet on In Court Woods:
I like to enter Court Woods by the path which rises from the little carpark at the corner of Walton Road and Norton's Wood Lane. Some of the paths are steep and stony and one of the main broad paths has been blocked by a tree stump since a section is no longer safe. After pausing on the log seat at the top of the ridge, I usually circle round the maze of paths, looking down on Clevedon Court and groaning at the noise of the motorway, emerging at the gateway by All Saint's Church. This gateway can be used as the entrance to the woods for easier walks on the broad paths but there are a few steps to be negotiated at first.

Woodland Wandering

On a rounded corner off Walton Road
Is an ancient Somerset CC sign
That wraps its arms around a telegraph pole
Wander Nortons Wood Lane way
Where ivy camouflages miles of wall
Built by extinct Lord Elton workmen
A wall only just holding back Court Wood's
Ambition to reclaim the road

Backs and fronts of houses
Allotments where gardeners engage
With woodland creatures
In a war on want with their crops
The wall plays hide and seek
Now hedge, now wall
While town houses run into open fields
And cottages huddle on roadsides

Passing by some big boulders
Once torn from the hillside, now
Standing guard at their old quarry entrance
Enjoy gardens, fields, dark wooded slopes
Horses grazing, that may
want to pass the time of day

Before reaching Harley Lane
Observe a bridleway on your right
Enter the rock strew gorge between
Moss covered wall and towering trees
Discover the many paths striking off here and there
Faintly delineated or well-trodden leafy ways
Merge with the 'Gordano Round' path
Which runs along the top of mapped contour lines
Giving views over the Gordano Valley
As it tiptoes past the Keeper's Cottage
Finally tumbling you out at All Saints Church
And almost back to the start.

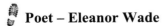 **Poet – Eleanor Wade**

Clevedon Court

Location on map .. *9*

Court to Camp

From silent church, the path ascends through pillars
carved from rock
Beneath a verdant canopy, where poets once took stock
The footsteps follow Tennyson and Thackeray,
Coleridge too
Their words still hang upon the air, with meaning found
anew

Upon the lawn above the Court, where Eltonware was
born
The walker stands to catch the view, now by the
highway torn
The sounds of traffic heading West intrude upon the
breeze
The only harsh discordant note among magnolia trees

And then the way heads up the rise, past quarries
overgrown
Where Clevedon villas started life from palely golden
stone
Through bluebell woods on sunlit track, where squirrels
dash and dart
And colours wait at every turn to sing out Nature's art
Then down to cross the M5 bridge above the deep
ravine
As horses and their riders walk, by all but few unseen
The echo of the hooves rings out, as far beneath those
spans

Like lemmings rush unceasing tides of cars and caravans.

The path winds on through woodland shade along the bridle trail

Until a vista opens out beyond a wooden rail

Grasses spread with buttercups, daisies and yellow vetch

Speedwell blue and orchids rare across the meadows stretch.

At last the climb to ancient fort above the green spread moor

Where long forgotten seas swept in, pushed by the tidal bore

The grassy battlements survive upon their earthen ramp

Amid the ghosts of early men, who once strode Cadbury Camp.

 Poet – Peter Gibbs

Clevedon Pottery

From the pots of blue-lined greyness
Cross the centuries speeds the call
To the bards of Lakeland verses
To the love that conquers all

Here they spent warm sunlit hours
'Fore the poppy stole their smiles
Led them cruelly into madness
Turned their high hopes into guiles

Now the clay shaped in the valley
Of the cleft where Romans strode
Hand-craft turned to gleaming beauty
Taps the poets' mother lode

Dragonflies and brush-stroke wildfowl
Wing across the bright-glazed skies
Cockerels crow to greet the dawning
Joy's reborn with each sunrise

Scents of violets and sweet myrtle
Gently waft through wooded vales
Soft and mild the whisper breezes
Aeolian chords from Celtic Wales
Who can say where springs the magic
Don't dissect the why and how
Just be glad to share the wonder
Celebrate the here and now.

 Poet – Peter Gibbs

The Triangle

Location on map .. *10*

Soft Saturday

Soft Saturday a-walking
Along the footpaths down
That wind from misty wooded heights
To vintage Clevedon Town

Accompanied by birdsong
The lovers hand in hand
Pass green-hued walls of ancient rocks
That spring forth from the land
Their glimpses of Swiss Valley
From high up Strawberry Hill
Are shared with just the privileged few
Who wander through the still
'Neath secret bluebell-smothered banks
And root-uncovered trees

They descend gently to the shops
That wait their whims to please
'Cross Highdale Road, o'er stone-carved stile
Past cottage gardens neat
They trace the hidden way towards
The busy bustling street

The tile-encircled Clocktower
Stands sentinel above
And balustrades of civic pride
Bear witness to their love.

 Poet – Peter Gibbs

The Undefeated

The defeated are hung
In history
And featured in BBC docu-dramas.

Yet the cider-scented
Vision did not die
With farm labourers hung at Kenn.

The fire
Set by suffragettes
At Old Church
Flames still.

Then there's the Consty.
Occupied in 1983;
An un-televised revolution,
Unforgotten.

And the Liberal Club.
Green fields captured
By a female army:
A Woman's Right to Cues.

The undefeated
Walk among us.
Through the Triangle,
Along Hill Road,
Down by the pier.
Every day.

 Howard Roderic Davies.

Note from the poet on The Undefeated:
Locations/events —
Kenn/Kenn Road: the Kenn hangings, England's last 'scene of crime' execution where three young farm labourers were hung in 1830.
Old Church/St Andrews: in 1914, suffragettes attempted to burn down Clevedon's Norman church during the 'Votes for Women' campaign.
The 'Consty'/Clevedon Conservative/Constitutional Club, Kenn Road: in 1983, the Club was occupied by protesters opposed to Margaret Thatcher's policies.
The Liberal Club (later the Triangle Club), north side of Triangle Clock: in the early 80s, it was occupied by a Clevedon Women's Group in protest at women being denied use of the billiard tables.

The Curzon

Location on map .. *11*

Top Gun '86

We huddled outside the cinema
giggled like schoolgirls

inside we held hands
groping for our seats in the dark

clutched popcorn bags tightly
mesmerised by the Tomcats

watched him strut in his uniform
tight pants and gleaming white teeth

we swooned and gasped
at his *inverted* manoeuvre

then practiced the *birdie*
with our ice creams

that night I named my cat Maverick
my friend named hers Goose

became huge Otis Redding fans
and wore fake dog tags to school

on Clevedon Pier we let our legs dangle
sang Sitting on the Dock of the Bay

like an old record player
over and over

 Poet – Tina M Edwards

'Dear Old Clevedon' my mum used to say,
as we sat on her favourite seat,
high above Ladye Bay.
The far off Welsh hills,
stood out proud and clear,
And as we gazed towards the west,
there lay that slender pier.
Victorian engineers made it,
they used strong Barlow Rails,
laid around the world,
from Sydney to South Wales,

We moved from Bristol to Clevedon in 1953,
and into an apartment high above the sea,
From our garden I'd oft look down on the pier,
and wait, baited breath, for the Bristol Queen to appear.
Oh those happy times, to Ilfracombe for the day,
or maybe cruise on around steep-cliffed Woody Bay.
Then sail home, a golden sun path on the sea,
And down to the galley with fish and chip tea.

Such sunny memories of my boyhood fun,
playing in Alexandra Gardens while out shopping with
mum.
There was Feltham's the fishmonger,
his marble slab full of 'fruits de mere'
While looking down from a hook, lifeless pheasants
would stare,
Mr Maynard kept The Creamery with sweets and ices
for sale,
Rotund and white coated, hearty and hale,
Mr Bull kept the pet shop,
sawdust sweet on the air,
And at his menagerie we boys would stare.

Our town had a coal yard and gasometers too,
And a railway where steam loco whistles blew,
as they ran clackity clack to Yatton and back.
The old Clevedon Mercury,
overlooking Six Ways,
supplied the town with its news,
back in those golden days.

So much has changed yet so much still gives joy
For the prom's leaning tree,
leaned when I was a boy.
And the bandstands still there,
and the Marine Lake too.
Used every day by the hardy few,
It will all still be there for many a day
so dear old Clevedon
I can still say.

   Poet – Nigel Heath

www.clevedoncommunitybookshop.coop